# Shopping Poems

## Compiled by John Foster

D1151096

## Contents

Shopping list  *Julie Holder*  2
Wrong trolley  *Eric Finney*  4
Whoops!  *Judith Nicholls*  6
Shopping  *Richard James*  7
Play shop  *Celia Warren*  8
The corner shop  *Richard James*  10
Chips for tea  *Margaret Rose*  12
At the toyshop  *John Foster*  14
1p short  *Julie Holder*  16

**Acknowledgements**

The Editor and Publisher wish to thank the following who have kindly given permission for the use of copyright material:

Eric Finney for 'Wrong trolley' © 1995 Eric Finney; John Foster for 'At the toyshop' © 1995 John Foster; Julie Holder for '1p short' and 'Shopping list' both © 1995 Julie Holder; Richard James for 'Shopping' and 'The corner shop' both © 1995 Richard James; Judith Nicholls for 'Whoops!' © 1995 Judith Nicholls; Margaret Rose for 'Chips for tea' © 1995 Margaret Rose; Celia Warren for 'Play shop' © 1995 Celia Warren.

# Shopping list

We went to the bakers
For bread and for buns.

We went to the fruit shop
For apples and plums.

We went to the butchers
For sausages and ham.

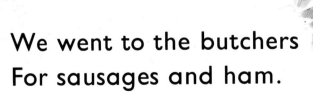

2

We went to the grocers
For butter and jam.

We went to the paper shop
For a comic for me.

Then we went to the café
For orange juice and tea.

*Julie Holder*

# Wrong trolley

Mum, there's catfood in our trolley
And we haven't got a cat!
There's a big bag of potatoes
And we didn't load up that.
Do you remember loading beans
Or peas or cauliflowers?
Mum, I know we're pushing it
But is this trolley ours?

*Eric Finney*

4

# Whoops!

Our supermarket keeps baked beans
inside a plastic bin.
They used to pile them on the floor
till James picked up the BOTTOM tin!

*Judith Nicholls*

## Shopping

If I could choose the shopping
We'd need lots of extra trolleys
To fill with all my favourite things
Like ice-cream
And spaghetti rings
And frozen orange lollies.

*Richard James*

## Play shop

With plastic pounds and pennies
and play-dough cakes and sweets,
it's not the sort of shop
you'd find in real streets.

Sweet

In between the play house
and the sand and water tray,
this shop is in the classroom
where the shoppers only play.

*Celia Warren*

shop

## The corner shop

It sells apples, green and red,
It sells poppadoms and bread,
It sells comics, it sells coffee,
It sells envelopes and toffee,
It sells carrots, it sells cheese,
It sells stamps and frozen peas,
It sells noodles, it sells string,
It sells every single thing.

*Richard James*

# Chips for tea

I'm off down the chip shop.
I've got my 50p.
Mum said I could get some
I'll have them for my tea.

I'll eat them from the paper,
Not bother with a plate.
Chips with salt and vinegar.
Smell them! Aren't they great!

*Margaret Rose*

# At the toyshop

I've saved up my money.
I've got three pounds to spend.
I'm looking for a present
For my best friend.

I'm going round the toyshop
To see what I can find.
I don't know what to buy her.
I can't make up my mind.

A puzzle game? Some felt-tips?
A plastic jumbo jet?
There's so much to choose from.
I don't know what to get.

I've saved up my money.
I've got three pounds to spend
To buy a birthday present
For my best friend.

*John Foster*

# 1p short

I had ten pence to spend,
I bought a chew
A jelly curl
A liquorice bootlace
A marshmallow whirl
A sherbet lemon
A bubble-gum
And had to borrow
1p from Mum.

*Julie Holder*

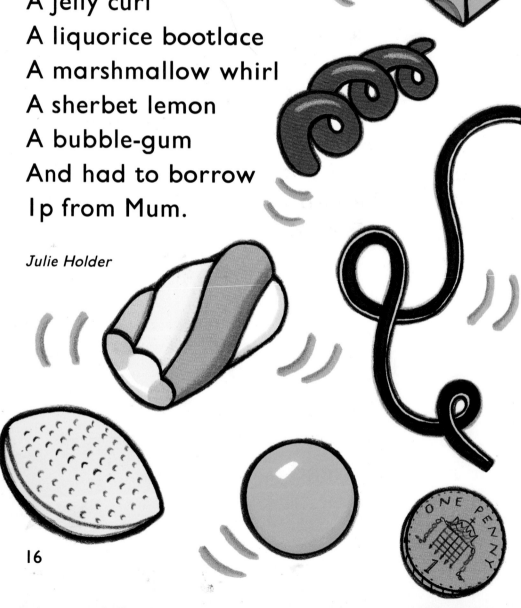